THE END OF AMERICAN FREEDOM

Free Speech Can Die in the 2020 Presidential Election

T.H. Logwood

"It is said that, 'Liberty dies with resounding applause.'"

THE LAST ELECTION

The 2020 Presidential election may well be the last free election we have in this country. Our liberties and rights are slipping away with every election cycle, and soon, our freedom of speech (expressed through our vote) may disappear. Once our ability to speak freely is gone, then all of our other rights will be silenced as well.

Strong words and a bold statement, but it may be very true as we watch and wrestle with the political and legal events as these weeks and months lead up to this key event in America. Watching the 2018 midterm elections, the trend and precursor for the next is clear. Rather, the trend is scary. Opinion surveys and many commentators suggest that socialism and socialistic ideals are acceptable, and even desirable, particularly with younger adults. If the next generation, our youth and young adults, are so swayed by the promises of "free stuff" and "the government will take care of you", then we are in grave danger indeed.

Remember the 2018 mid-term election? What was at stake, and who showed up to vote? The rhetoric and saber-rattling from both the republican and democratic sides, coupled with the endless blabbering dribble from the bias media, spelled out clearly the goals of the democrat party. The independent voters decided the vote, and the preservation of this country's liberties continues. But for how much longer?

At stake, according to the pro-republican stance, was stability and legality. Under the strong leadership of President Trump, the economy has blossomed to an unfathomable growth rate around 4% (give or take a smidge) almost immediately after he took office. He kept his campaign promises of bringing at least one (now two) "Originalist" supreme court justices to the bench, repealed burdensome and ridiculous government regulations, restored the rule of law (especially with regards to immigration), prevented disastrous world conflicts such as with North Korea, upheld constitutional rights and principles, affirmed the right to life and the right to bear arms, among many other bold actions. The republican platform was to keep moving in this direction, build on job growth and the economy, following the "rule of law", fix the illegal alien and immigration mess, and restore civility among our divided peoples.

Now without question, the democrat side clearly fought for the opposite platform. I say clearly, because there was never a single mention of policy, or what they would do to improve the lives of Americans. They took a different approach, and showed truly what the new party stood for. Their intent was to unravel and destroy every positive action President Trump has accomplished.

They yelled out hate-speech towards anything of growth, improvement, or prosperity. They shouted about impeaching the newly appointed justice to the supreme court. Many in congress writhed with hatred and made idle threats of impeaching President Trump himself. These elected democrats cried and had temper-tantrums about anything related to the mass invasion by illegal aliens. Never once, did any democrat candidate talk about "How" they would fix health care, restore jobs for Americans, do better with our international responsibilities, and so on. Ok, if you are unhappy with a policy or action, tell us in clearly, without the emotional drama, of "what" you would do. Their entire political strategy was to slander and malign anyone and everything that was that contrary to their hate-filled dialogue. Even the mainstream media, heavily biased against the president, was in lock-step with the democrat mob mentality. Is the new democrat party truly representative of all democrats?

AND WHO SHOWED UP TO VOTE?

"It's that time again, elections." To some it's dread and bother, a disruption in the daily routine, so too many people just don't vote. To others, it is an opportunity for gain and advancement, propelling an agenda, or other ends. Whatever the motives, or lack of motives, the bottom line is this, we have a Right and a privilege to choose leaders in this country. Our Right is different than in most other countries in the world, because our election process is still free from the interference of government. Not many nations of the world can claim that. Certainly there is graft and corruption, and the lobbying of special interests that can influence "how" we vote, but the process itself is still relatively the same as our founding fathers intended it long ago.

In the 2018 mid-term election cycle, the democrats made a strong showing, with a fairly high voter turnout. What the party had done very well, was to mobilize their campaigns, with workers and volunteers, that actively encouraged people to vote. Overall, the democrat machine was well tuned, enthusiastic, and passionate, resulting in a good turnout. Despite some of the questionable tactics and methods to get people registered and voted, "the process" of promoting the freedom to vote earns the party a resounding "Kudos". The exit polling showed a very strong young adult block, but decreased voting from the African-American group, and Hispanic voters.

Mid-aged suburban white women seemed to strongly support the republican candidates, as did increased voters among the Black and Hispanic communities. It is quite likely that many voters were encouraged to vote "against" the constant maligning of the Kavanaugh appointment, many being former democrats. The greatly improved job situation also prompted minorities to "vote red". The traditional white male voter backbone of the republican party actually was down from the 2016 presidential election. Overall, the republicans were weak and pathetic in many of the races. They were slow and lacking in messaging, showed little passion, and the underlying sentiment was, "who cares". The results were appalling for a party that gained so much just two years earlier when they elected Trump, the Outsider.

The importance of your vote, which is your voice, should be expressed, even now, and especially for this upcoming election. If you can physically do so, do vote. Whether you like a particular candidate or party, or a proposed law that's on a ballot, let your voice be heard. You have the right not to vote, and that is a free decision for you to determine. But not to vote, is surrendering your voice to the outcome of those that did cast their ballots.

As our society writhes with turmoil and unrest, the forces of change come about, heading towards a revolution or major upheaval of our liberties. And in this country, at this moment in time, many of these groups, will further seek to undermine our rights to vote, our power to voice our opinion, and that would sound the death-blow to America. If our speech (and the choices made through voting) are restricted or controlled by laws and deceitful leaders, then the path to a socialistic and then totalitarian country will be complete.

VOTING IS A RIGHT
AND PRIVILEGE

Vote, or not, it is your decision, but it far more important than you can imagine. It is your Right, and duty, as a citizen to change the face of the governing bodies, if you so choose. The process of voting came about in this country because of the forced hand of the English crown to dictate almost every facet of the lives of the colonial governed.

In the new land, the New World, the colonies were largely established to be free of the dictates of their rulers in England. It was often related to spiritual choice and expression, that led groups to the new world seeking some relief from the overlords of government interference with their beliefs and speech, especially when contrary to government actions. The new land meant a certain amount of liberty to express thoughts and ideas, and the election process if not borne, was greatly fostered.

It was greatly due to the interference of the governing bodies in the daily affairs of the colonists, which dissention grew and eventually turned to rebellion, hence the revolution of liberty had come about. Authority over our lives is contrary to our innate sense of freedom and independence.

The founding fathers were absolutely brilliant in their crafting of the constitution, especially in regards to setting up the system of voting. They clearly understood what it meant to have a voice, to be able to freely express an opinion or idea without being arrested or suppressed by those in power. Certainly there are great dissertations of how the system of voting came about, but the point being, it did, and is meant so the common man (now including women) can have some say in how their lives would be governed.

THE CONSTITUTION

Nicely written and clearly defined in the remarkable document, the US Constitution is nothing short of a miraculous template of how to govern a people. Now, one of the chief cornerstones of the constitution, and basic law of the land, is that there are to be periodic elections, free from government interference, for the people to select among themselves the next body of leaders. That is, freely held elections for various offices and levels of government, free from the coercion or compulsion by the government or other persons.

Without this privilege, there is no liberty. It takes time back to the pre-revolutionary days where the government would control what you said, what you did, and all other aspects of life. Without the freedom to choose for ourselves, there is no incentive to improve ones life. Power in the hands of a few elites, has never worked out well for any country, throughout all of human history. What happens in every nation, documented throughout history, is that power corrupts. As power becomes concentrated in the hands of a few, they abuse it. Then the rulers oppress the people. Finally, due to opposition, the rulers mass murder their own citizens to maintain their power. Gratefully, our Founders divided the centers of powers, each as a check upon the other.

A people that are free to decide for themselves are happier in their daily lives, more productive, which makes the nation great and prosperous as a whole. That is it in a nutshell, a free people are happier and more productive. And that is the intent of the constitution.

On the federal level, the founding fathers intended that the government's primary role and duty was to provide for the common defense of the nation, and, support the common good. Without defense of the nation, when needed, such as by a foreign invader, then a nation is overrun and destroyed. The Founders understood this all too well in those early times, so in a simplistic but exacting manner, they crafted the document to make provisions for the armed and legal protections for the country. This included, if you study the document, for maintaining and defending the borders. A nation has the sovereign Right to have borders, which is the governments top priority.

Along with national defense, the Founders tried to instill the idea that if people are left to their own means, they will create jobs and businesses (commerce), for which families and society can provide for their own needs, hence a healthier country. With increased governmental interference in the lives of people, happiness and productivity declines. So the document intended to be in support of the "good works" that people would do, rather than government controlling the daily aspects of life. "The pursuit of happiness" as it reads, means for the government to not interfere with the lives of the people. Laws and rules certainly are needed to govern and maintain the rights and liberties of society, but not into every decision of our personal lives.

Now over two hundred years later, the heavy hand of government has burdened us all with endless regulations, restrictions, and controls, impeding the happiness and contentment of the governed. Granted, as our society has changed and developed, a certain amount of governmental control is obviously necessary, but as the government continues to grow, the bureaucracy has strangled many of our rights and privileges, including our freedom of speech.

THE POLITICAL DIVIDE

Today, right now in America, there are groups that are trying to prevent your freedom of speech to be heard. There are many forces at work to strip away the rights and freedoms we hold, that are sanctioned by our constitutional foundations. Should I name them? They are in every slanderous news and media agency, half of the current governing body, and the various groups shouting and pillaging as they attempt to suppress thought.

Yes, speak out, let your voice be heard with truth or opposing thoughts, but without oppression. That is, if we are adults, let us discuss and reason as adults. When one shouts and fusses, then it is that inner child that needs a "time-out", or maybe a spanking. If you don't have anything substantive to offer, then screaming and potty-mouth babble will never sway a debate. For many in our media and leadership roles, they act more like nasty children, than people we should follow or admire.

*"When all else fails - scream
the race card"*

If you disagree with their thinking, these zombie groups will shout you down, or take legal and sometimes violent actions to silence thought. Watching groups or mobs march down the streets crying and wailing as they throw rocks and destroy property, screaming hateful insults, really does not help their cause.

How many news stories and reports have been just that, mob violence. As elections get closer, the divisive rhetoric and violence increases. Is that the new normal for American expression or speech?

It is fair to disagree and oppose the thoughts and ideas of someone else, that is our liberty. If you don't want to listen, that is your right. If you disagree, that is your right. If you want to speak to the contrary and try to persuade others in thinking the same, that is your right also. But is there a line that cannot or should not be crossed? Yes. When you limit and prevent someone else from their rights, that must not happen. Your right is to speak freely, without governmental interference, or other parties suppressing your voice. That is how our fundamental laws work. The rule of law tells us, that "one persons rights end when it interferes with another's".

If there is an alternate or opposing viewpoint on a subject, then "can we not sit down together and reason?" In a society where media and a wide diversity of peoples and opinions abound, there should be great ideas and discussions of every topic and idea to enrich and improve our lives. What we see is the contrary, where the media is controlled by biased deceitful owners and executives (zombie masters), that seek revenues by a ratings ranking systems, hence controlling what the public will view. It is money that drives the media, emotions that fuels the information presented, and the control of free and open speech is the result.

The freedom of speech relates exactly to the freedom and right to vote. If your vote elects leaders that uphold the rule of law, then they are apt to uphold the free dissemination of speech. If you are prevented from voting, intimated, threatened with violence or governmental control, your rights to speak out, through the casting of a vote, is wrong. It is a violation of the most basic of American freedoms, and that must never be allowed to happen.

If poor leaders are elected to office, then they will enact more laws and regulations to limit your freedom of expression, even voting. And what was the basic of all basic American privileges, becomes a memory. With every regulation and law that limits what we can and can not do as a free people, then our liberties disappear. We as a people sink into the historical abyss of government controlling everything, and there is no more freedom. This is also exactly true of every right and freedom guaranteed by our constitution.

THE NEW DEMOCRAT PARTY

The new democrat party aligns itself to bold speech with no substance. Violent and divisive rhetoric to stir up the masses of brainwashed supporters to overthrow society, on every issue of tradition, law, and freedoms. The new party professes the goodness of socialistic ideals, but white-washes the realities of repeated historical failures. Condemnation without solution. The peoples party is no longer the party of the people, but by the party leadership is pushing to overturn the rights of free speech, rule of law, equality for all. They are indoctrinating of our school children with the idea that "government provides" versus hard work and achievement by merit. This is fact.

This radical departure of party norms relates exactly to every election, where more and more districts and States are turning blue. Turning blue, not by advancing sound policies and programs to make positive changes (as they offer none), but more so accomplished through unrealistic ideals. The general populace is being brainwashed by empty rhetoric that touts restriction and control, unsubstantiated opinion over logic and reason, yet the vote turns blue, more and more. The power of the individual is given over to mass hysteria.

If this country is to be changed, let it be changed, but through the process of law as it was founded. But what is changed, may not be what is good or right, or even fair. And what changes, is not easily changed back. If traditions are deemed wrong, and what we have previously known as failed ideologies become entrenched as doctrine. Then individual liberties are restricted, the rule of law becomes contrary to those established by our forefathers, and power becomes concentrated in the hands of a few.

And power in the hands of a few, ruins nations. It is said, that power leads to a hunger for more, like any addictive drug. Once those who thirst for power instead of service, attain power, they start to abuse it. As the abuse and corruption increases, then oppression of opposition begins. And the historical factual reality is then, citizens are mass murdered by their own government. Look at every socialist or totalitarian country, and count the bodies. In recent times, just look at Nazi Germany, Cambodia under Paul Pott, Argentina, many nations within Africa and South America, everywhere. Power corrupts, and the only way to stop the opposition is to remove them. That is the historical reality in every case.

Who, or what groups adhere to what you hold as good and right? What you believe in, and the rights and privileges you enjoy, are just a few votes away from being changed. Think for yourself, and decide in the way that works best for you. Align yourself with those that hold those principles and ideals you want. It doesn't matter which party, just learn who the candidates are, and support those that have the values and principles you value.

THE HATE TRUMP MOVEMENT

One of the great things this country offers, is the election cycle. By constitutional law, this country is to have free and fair elections, whereby the governed will periodically elect its leaders from their peers. And for the most part, for over 200 years, our system of elections and voting is fairly honest. The outcomes are sometimes a question, and when one side loses, they lick their wounds, get on with business, and plan for the next election. At least, that is how it should be.

Remember the 2016 presidential election? It turned a new chapter in American politics, where the outsiders were favored over the mainstream candidates. It was also characterized by hate-speech, threats, temper-tantrums, protest marches, and a bias inflammatory media spreading yellow journalism the likes of which parallels re-war Nazi Germany. The democrats could not stand the fact, literally the fact, that Donald J. Trump was elected president, over their deceptive and depraved failure in Ms. Clinton.

Who is Donald J. Trump anyways? Outsider, businessman, real estate tycoon, playboy, TV star, republican, moderate conservative, a disrupter of the status quo, and a nationalist. Who in their right mind would have ever guessed that "he" would become president, leader of the free world, defender of the Constitution, and for now, has brought a halt to the national decay this country has had. Against all odds, he won, and the leftist party of the democrats hasn't accepted this reality, even to this very moment. And they never will.

Not only the democrats, but the republican rhinos and never-Trumpers, the entrenched swamp rats of the DC power cesspool, all have been against him ever since his announcement to run for president. It isn't just a dislike for the president, but hatred as for everything that he is, and stands for. These are the power-hungry wanna-be leaders, seeking to control the masses with their own sick propaganda of one worldism and global control. They have been seeking power and control for decades now, with the aim of destroying the constitution and all of the freedoms granted therein.

Even in the political volleying today, over the border wall and security, the most vile and deceptive leaders, Pelosi and Schumer, have shown what's in their hearts, hatred. They have a hatred towards the president, hatred of the constitution, hatred of truth and fairness, and hatred of the free people that side with the president. If politics and the control of the masses is more important than doing what is right and best for the nation, then those types of leaders need to be voted out of office. Are the democrat leaders we want in office? Do they serve the people, or cause harm?

President Trump is not the issue, it's what he has done and what he hopes to accomplish that the Trump-Haters oppose. Those things are the Constitution, the rule of law, enforcing the laws, rights and liberties. In a society where government holds the power and makes decisions on behalf of the people, free speech is not tolerated, the good of the people is marginalized, the health and productivity of the nation is stifled. "Power held in the hands of a few, will bring ruin to a nation."

SLAVERY IN AMERICA

Throughout human societies, power and control over others is a dark side of our nature. Hence slavery, or the compulsion and control over other people has been a plague not easily cured. America started its young Statehood with slave ownership as a normal part of daily life. Through the struggles of history and blood, the ownership over people had been stopped by constitutional decree. But has it really?

According to studies and reports of world activities on the subject of slavery, there are about 40 nations that practice and allow the ownership of people. America is on that list. The idea of slavery is not just physical ownership, but also through control. Someone who is controlled by another, is that not also slavery, or a form thereof? Control is the drug of the powerful. Throughout history, it was those in power, the rich, the government, the military, and the politicians, that made the rules and laws to control people. Some rules are for the benefit of society as a whole, other regulations are made to increase or hold the power of the elite class. As groups or leaders grow in power, the end result is control. Control leads to restriction, and restriction more often is of rights and liberties, leading to eventual slavery.

Which is which can be determined by the constitution, although the interpretation for modern application becomes debatable. If not stated or with precedence, then a law or ruling may be impeding on our rights. As that pertains to voting, for instance, does that restrict our freedom of speech? What about voter ID laws? Perhaps necessary in the dishonest world we live in, but one can argue that it is a way to restrict that right.

In America today, there are news stories where people are held against their will as slaves (often for personal pleasures), but for the most part, slavery as we define it, is very rare. Not absent in this country, news stories do arise about slavery. It is reasonable to argue that there are other forms of slavery being widely practiced in this country, such as by the banks. If you are in debt, you work as a slave to the bank to try and pay back what is owed. Financial slavery might be considered a type of control over people. Those who struggle with addictions are slaves to that control source. Governmental control by rules and regulations, may not quite be considered slavery, but as more of our rights get stripped away, then we are becoming slaves under legal means.

Look at the various debates and controversies mentioned today, and ponder whether our rights are being threatened, or society is positively fostered. Are our freedoms and liberties enhanced or preserved as guaranteed by our founding Fathers, or restricted by laws crafted by leaders or groups.

To be bold, look at many of the subjects people talk about. How about marriage and legal relationships? Do laws restrict or enhance "the pursuit of happiness"? If ones actions does not infringe upon anothers' right, then constitutionally, maybe it's fine. Do voter laws suppress your right to vote? What would be fair and reasonable to assure "fair and free" elections? Are hate-speech laws lawful? What would constitute "hate", a differing opinion? Too much is being litigated these days because a group or persons finds "offense" or "bad feelings" because of the words of another person. Talk is talk, but when it comes to laws, that sounds more like the suppression of free speech.

How about gun laws and restricting the Right to bear arms? The intent of the Founders was to assure that the people would be able to defend themselves and their families from harm, and, to oppose a government that was unjust (tyrannical according to the document). Any infringement made by government is a violation of our rights. Don't accept the lies argued to the contrary. The Bill of Rights has this as the number two in importance for a reason, it's important.

Here also, religious teachings are also in the center of controversy these days. Speech and religion are the first and most important rights the founders declared. Why, that was what the English rulers suppressed most. You must not restrict free thought or personal preference of spiritual worship. That also includes the fight over abortion. What is life, the handling of "the pursuit of happiness" in conflict with religious belief, speech, and law? Laws are words spoken by men. Some are for the good of the nation and its citizens, others are for power and gain. When government enacts laws to restrict either speech or religion, that is wrong.

Important to note, there are great lengths happening right now in this country to control these rights, and that spells the end of American liberty, and ushers in the destruction of this nation. Watch and glean from every news story, every speech made, every law and action taken, to see if our freedoms are being upheld or restricted.

ABOUT LOSING
OUR LIBERTIES

Is it possible to lose our Constitutional rights and freedoms? These are guaranteed under the law, aren't they? Yes, but no.

With each election, it results in more radical thinking politicians taking office, by which they get laws and regulations passed to silence free speech, for instance. Not so long ago, one could talk openly of another person or a group of people, have heated opposing debate, but that now is limited by "hate speech laws" and other controls. Yes, for sure it is not nice or kind to talk ill of another person or group, but can we not speak what's on our mind anymore? What if you spoke against a government agency or a governmental employee? Laws are being passed to limit what you can say against the government. What was accountability of government by the people, laws are starting to restrict that opposition, and then bring about serious consequences. The silencing of open discussion, debate, or defiance, is control of our liberty. Some politicians seek more control over us by enacting more laws and regulations in every area of our lives. Learn who the candidates are before you vote. Does the party platform, their set of ideals, align with your own, and how you want to live?

If democrat politicians (who have the mission to control the lives of the people) are elected, they will enact laws to reduce or eliminate the rights and privileges we hold, in particular our freedom to speak in opposition, our rights to bear arms, and so on. As we lose our freedom of speech (again as an example), we become slaves to the government.

Don't the republicans seek control also? Yes, sure they do, as all who are elected are subject to the lusts of power and control. It's just that in recent times, the democrat party has become so radical in their quest to control people by restrictive laws and regulations. Is that right or even fair? Some think it's fine, others are less happy, but the movement towards a socialist and totalitarian slavery will end the liberties and freedoms we still have.

This trend in our elections and the types of people elected to office is actually very scary. Too many are pushing for a government led, governmental controlled society. All countries that have embraced that style of slavery, are unproductive, with a people that are unhappy. Those nations, historically, have not remained very long.

OTHER FREEDOMS
TO LOSE

Freedom to speak out and speak freely, is not the only right and freedom we can lose, but all of the others as well.

Gun rights are greatly threatened too. The Second Amendment protects the citizens' right to bear arms, for personal and family protection, but also to stand against tyrannical rulers. This fight has escalated in recent years, flamed by the biased media, and outspoken elitists. Here too, the critics claim that having guns is unsafe, yet those individuals have armed security and walled homes.

We have plenty of good Gun laws in effect, but not adhered to in most states. Rather than add new laws to restrict gun owner-ship, how about enforce the current laws? For example, the background check laws for gun purchasing was developed with the assistance of the NRA. The way it is suppose to work, is that criminal offenders are suppose to have their names and information submitted by the state and local levels into the NCIC database. From there, everyone with access to the system can then approve or deny a purchase via the information submitted. Therein lies the rub, information has to be submitted into the system, which is done at the state or and local levels. Not to do so, makes the whole background checking system incomplete due to the lack of relevant data. It is a good law and a good system, if it were used as intended.

Also, beware the "Red Hat" laws. Many states are implementing what is called Red Hat laws, whereby any person can accuse another person of being "dangerous". This then triggers law enforcement to confiscate that accused persons' firearms. Based on merely hearsay, without proof, and without due process. Is that not a violation of many of our personal rights and freedoms? Yes, and it is yet another way the leftists are starting to "void" the Second Amendment.

Like every argument the leftists scream about, they hold themselves above the law, and often not adhering to their own arguments. They are hypocrites.

As you look at the history of every nation that has turned socialist, the first thing the government would do is to remove the guns. Remove the ability of the citizens to fight against injustice, and the people will be easily controlled. Remove the guns, and all other rights and freedoms can not be defended. Again, take Nazi Germany for example. There was strong active opposition to the rise of the socialists, but once the guns were seized, the Nazis eliminated all of the critics. And we are talking about the government killing its own citizens. It is that scary.

Freedom of religious worship? Our Judeo-Christian roots that bore this country and our entire legal system, has been greatly under attack as well. We are free to worship whom and what we like, or nothing at all, without the interference of government mandating what we can do. The idea of "separation of Church and State", has been grossly portrayed by those seeking to abolish Christianity. Thomas Jefferson and Hamilton had written about this matter from the beginning, citing that "not separation, but rather that "government shall not impose a religion". In other words, government would not declare a State religion. Being a person of faith, whatever you believe, and part of the government structure, should not be an issue. It is, and watching every

Supreme Court nomination hearing, and even most Cabinet level screenings, there are those people, mostly the democrats, that scream about the separation of Church and State. Having a person that holds a belief and moral compass in public office is a good thing. Look at the corrupt lying filth currently serving in office, and then decide which is better.

Abortion is Legalized Murder

And what about "the right to life"? The abortion question, is not just a freedom of religious worship, but it is also a freedom of speech. Perhaps the greater overall question is whether it is right and lawful for the government to kill, or sanction the killing, of its own citizens. Although the Supreme Court allowed the ability to kill unborn babies as a rule of law in Roe vs. Wade, is it right? No, it is a disgusting and abhorrence to everything good and honorable that this country touts to be. Murder is murder. An unborn child is still a human being, up until now.

The State of New York and Vermont have passed new laws allowing the death of babies right up until the child takes its first breath. And, the voting assembly members applauded the new law with resounding glee! It is said that liberty will die with resounding applause. Are we there? Whether life begins at conception or when a baby draws its first breath, is irrelevant. The question is, how can we as a nation allow the murder of our own innocent and defenseless citizens? We are suppose to be a nation ruled by law, but not all laws are good or just. Where is the sanity of our lawmakers? This is murder, plain and simple.

Now if this hennas debauchery of injustice is not overruled, then the rights of free speech, religious worship, and "the pursuit of happiness", are made mute. Our freedoms as guaranteed under the US Constitution are destroyed. Those lawmakers, supporters of such legislation, and any group or organizations that adheres with such, are murders and co-conspirators. Is this country really going down this path? Then truth and justice in America is a lie!

What follows next? Well, because the murder of babies is made legal, the next step is to broaden that "definition" of whom can be (legally) murdered. Next will be young children no longer wanted by their parents, or perhaps the elderly will be killed at the whim of madmen. Then from there, any opposition group or segment of citizens, like white males, Christians, deplorable republicans, and so on, can face the death squads (by law). "When the sword is unsheathed, it is difficult to put it back without first spilling blood."

Here also, if and when the government is allowed to restrict your rights to own firearms, or takes them away completely, then there will be no more questions about religion, free speech, abortion, rights to assemble, protests against the government, and so on. Those who gain power will abuse it, then they will oppress the people, which then they will start murdering the citizenry. Strongly ponder these thoughts

MAKE A DIFFERENCE

Your vote does count. Your vote is your voice. It's a liberty and a right that must not be silenced or impeded by opposition, or by the government. To allow your voice to be shut down, you lose the one easy, and best, freedom a citizen can hold. "Use it or lose it", is a cliche sometimes used, and it is applicable now. Voting is your decision, take a stand, either "for" or "against", but voice your opinion, it does matter.

Our government was founded on the principle that if people are left to live their lives freely, society grows and prospers, supported by happy citizens. Creativity and invention, improvements of life, make for a better world. As simplistic as that sounds, basically it's true. Our system of government was designed and set up to assure the people would have the liberty to become all they can aspire to do. The freedom of free and open speech has been the cornerstone of the greatness this country has shared, rooted in the process of free and open elections. Every vote counts, and every citizen has a duty to make this country better, according to their own conscience.

The importance of your vote, which is your voice, should be expressed, even now, and especially for this upcoming election. If you can physically do so, do vote. As mentioned previously, whether you like a particular party or candidate, or a person seeking reelection, let your voice be heard. You right is also not to vote, which is your free decision. But , is surrendering your voice by not voting, is to submit to the will of someone else.

T. H. Logwood

As our society writhes with turmoil and unrest, forces of change come about, heading towards a revolution or major upheaval of our liberties. And in this country, at this moment in time, many people and groups, seek to undermine our rights to vote, our power of speech, all of our other freedoms and liberties we still have. That would sound the death-blow to America.

ABOUT THE AUTHOR

I grew up in a middle class family, had a father that worked, a mother that stayed home and raised children, the typical traditional American home. We had a small house, one car, (no) white picket fence, we had pets, regular schooling, church-goers, watched news and various TV shows, and had all of the cliche normal things in life typified during the 1950s and 60s. Life was normal and decent, reasonably peaceful, and safe.

My father was a veteran, worked a blue collar job, and was a straight-line democrat, just like his father before him. The Kennedy era thinking of party politics was pretty much his thinking as well. And for many decades, that seemed to work well in America. I too learned and adopted similar ideas of how life and government should work and coexist.

But that has changed radically over the past couple decades as the democrat party is no longer the party of the average working man. One would best describe the party as what we used to call the Communist-Socialist party during that earlier era. Now the party is all about hate speech, bigotry, division, dirty-politics, rampant dishonesty and deception by party leaders and candidates, and everything revolving around government control. This is no longer the democrat party America once loved.

The candidates and false narratives they promoted were enough to make me switch parties. Over the last many election cycles while the democrats drove further left, I pushed my family and friends to switch parties and vote further right. Not that the republicans are perfect by any means, but they do hold to more of the values and principles I do. The biggest area where they align with my own thinking are the ideas of limited government, a government hands-off ideology, and support of the Constitution and the foundations of this country. Upholding our rights and freedoms are more their forte, so this is where we will stay.

My hope is to share these thoughts with you, so that you can glean some insight of the struggle we face over our dying liberties. Thank you reading this.

www.ingramcontent.com/pod-product-compliance
Lightning Source LLC
Chambersburg PA
CBHW031922270726
48655CB00007BA/3137